LEMURS

LEMURS

Norman D. Anderson and Walter R. Brown

Illustrated with photographs

Dodd, Mead & Company
New York

1 2 3 4 5 6 7 8 9 10

Library of Congress Cataloging in Publication Data

Anderson, Norman D.
Lemurs.

Includes index.
Summary: Introduces the physical characteristics, habits, and natural environment of several kinds of lemurs whose principal home is the forest of Madagascar. Also discusses the uncertain future of these animals in the wild and what is being done to preserve them from extinction.
1. Lemurs—Juvenile literature. [1. Lemurs]
I. Brown, Walter R., 1929-   . II. Title.
QL737.P95A53   1984   599.8′1   84-8097
ISBN 0-396-08454-0

Contents

Chapter 1
Chiclette

This strange-looking animal is not "E.T." or some other creature from outer space. This is Chiclette. She was born on April 6, 1983, at Duke University's Primate Center in Durham, North Carolina. At birth she was smaller than a person's thumb.

Chiclette is a lemur. She and other lemurs are relatives of monkeys and apes.

Chiclette's mother, Yvette, was at least thirty years old when Chiclette was born. Very few lemurs live to be this old. Everyone at the Primate Center was surprised when Yvette gave birth to a baby so late in life.

Perhaps Chiclette was so tiny because her mother was

Chiclette, shortly after birth

so old. Most baby lemurs of her kind that are born at the Primate Center weigh around four ounces. Chiclette weighed less than one ounce. Hundreds of lemurs have been born at the Primate Center, but Chiclette was the smallest one of her kind yet. The scientists were not sure the tiny baby would live.

Yvette was so old that she could not produce milk for her new baby. So Chiclette was wrapped in a soft cloth and put into an incubator usually used for human babies. The scientists watched her closely. They fed her a mixture of milk and sugar through a tube for two weeks.

Although Chiclette was kept alive this way, she did not grow very much. Fortunately, one of her older sisters, named Nadia, adopted the little baby. Nadia had given birth to a normal-sized baby on April 19. She had plenty of milk for both babies. At that time, Chiclette weighed only a little more than one ounce. Nanette, the other baby lemur, was almost four times as heavy.

In spite of her poor start, Chiclette grew quickly. In six months she had nearly caught up with Nanette in size. They spent many happy hours playing together.

Nadia with the two lemur babies, Nanette (left) and Chiclette

Chiclette, like the other lemurs at the Primate Center, developed a "sweet tooth" for raisins.

Chiclette, Yvette, Nanette, and Nadia are collared lemurs. There are only fourteen of these beautiful little animals in the United States. All of them live at the Duke Primate Center.

When she is full grown, Chiclette may be larger than her mother. She should be about eighteen inches long,

from the tip of her pointed nose to the base of her bushy tail. She will probably weigh about five pounds.

Adult collared lemurs are covered with thick, dark brown or grayish-brown fur. They have dark-colored tails that are about the same length as their bodies. The tops of their heads and their ears are black in the case of males and gray in females. The long fur around the lower part of their faces is pale orange.

Collared lemurs, like Chiclette and her family, are just one of some twenty different kinds of lemurs. All lemurs have fur-covered bodies and most have quite long tails. Some look a bit like monkeys and are about the same size. Others are smaller and look more like mice or squirrels. Each of the different kinds of lemurs have differing patterns of fur color. In some cases, the males and females have different colors of fur.

Lemurs live in trees much of the time. They eat fruit and leaves and a few other kinds of food in the wild. Most kinds of lemurs are active in the daytime, but a few are active only at night. Lemurs are gentle, but inquisitive animals.

An adult male collared lemur

Scientists classify lemurs as primates. There are about 200 different kinds of primates, most of which live in trees. Most primates can grasp objects with their hands and feet, and have nails rather than claws. Their eyes are on the front of their heads. This allows them to look at an

object with both eyes at the same time and better judge distance.

Scientists divide primates into two groups. One group includes the monkeys, apes, and humans. The other group, called prosimians, includes the lemurs and primates such as lorises, pottos, and bush babies. These animals look a lot like lemurs and are related to them in about the same way wolves and foxes are related to dogs.

Chapter 2
Lemurs in the Wild

All of the wild lemurs in the world today live on the island of Madagascar and on a few nearby islands. Madagascar is the fourth largest island in the world. It is nearly 1,000 miles long and is 360 miles wide at one point.

Madagascar is a tropical island. It is only 220 miles from the southeastern coast of Africa. Some of the many mountains on the island are very high. The tops of some are nearly two miles above the ocean.

Lemurs once lived in many other parts of the world. But in Africa, Europe, and North America they had natural enemies. Other animals hunted and killed them.

Bigger and stronger primates, such as monkeys and apes, got most of the food, and the smaller lemurs could not compete. The forests in which they lived also slowly changed. All of the lemurs in the world, except for those on Madagascar and those few small islands nearby, slowly disappeared.

How the lemurs got to Madagascar is still a mystery. It may be that ancestors of today's lemurs floated to the

island from Africa. Perhaps storms threw trees and large branches into the sea, and the small primates clung to these until they reached dry land. This would have been millions and millions of years ago.

Lemurs found an ideal home on Madagascar. At that time, most of the island was covered with thick forests. And, except for a few large birds and crocodiles, there were no natural enemies to prey on the gentle little animals.

So the lemurs thrived in their new home. And over many millions of years, they slowly changed. Some came to have brightly colored fur and beautiful markings. Some kinds grew large, while others stayed small. Over about 50 million years, the lemurs changed until there were about forty different kinds living on Madagascar.

About 2,000 years ago, something happened to the lemurs' home on Madagascar. Humans arrived on the island. Now the lemurs on the island had enemies. The human beings hunted the lemurs for food. They also cut down the trees, in which the animals lived, to clear land for farming.

Area of Madagascar where trees were cut and other plants now cover the landscape

Today only a small area of the island of Madagascar is covered with trees. Most of these trees are found only along the coast. As the trees that provided homes and food disappeared, the lemurs began to die out, and several kinds have disappeared from the earth. They are gone forever, and we know about them only from fossils that have been found.

Much of Madagascar's forest area has been destroyed

Chapter 3
Ringtailed Lemurs

One of the best-known lemurs is the ringtailed lemur. Because of its very long tail that is marked with black and white rings, it is an unusual-looking animal that is popular in zoos.

Ringtails are about the size of a large cat when fully grown. Their bodies are about a foot long. They weigh about five pounds. Their fur is very thick. It is brownish-gray on the animal's back, and gray on the legs. The fur on the chest and stomach is nearly white. So is the fur on their cheeks, their large ears, and between their eyes. Black rings around the eyes make the ringtails look as if they are wearing masks.

The tails of ringtailed lemurs are somewhat longer than their bodies. The fur on their tails is long. When a group of ringtails is sitting in trees, their striped tails hang down and look a bit like huge, fuzzy caterpillars.

Ringtailed lemurs spend more time on the ground than do most other kinds of lemurs. It is not unusual to see a large group of these animals walking slowly along the ground. They can walk on their hind legs, waving their long, ringed tails in the air. The tails help the animals keep their balance. Lemurs cannot use their tails to hold onto branches, as monkeys do.

The male ringtail uses its tail in other ways. Sometimes a "stink fight" breaks out between two males. During a "stink fight," the animals draw their tails over glands near their wrists. They then flick the scented tails at rivals.

Male ringtails also leave their scent on trees. To do this, the animal stands on it hind feet and holds the tree trunk with both hands. It then scratches at the bark with rough spurs that grow on the insides of its wrists. This is a way of letting other ringtails know who was here, what

Ringtailed lemurs — mother and youngster — at Duke University's Primate Center

sex they were, and perhaps how old they are.

A troop of ringtails will be made up of about equal numbers of males and females—about seven to eight of each—with a group of children. The males are a little bigger and stronger than the females. But the females take first choice of food and a place to rest and sleep.

Each troop of ringtails feeds over a certain area of the forest. Most of the time they eat pods and leaves of the tamarind and other plants found in Madagascar. Once in a while they will pick a flower to munch on.

The troop usually moves in a certain way. The adult females will lead. Mature males and the young follow them. Bringing up the rear is a group of males not yet fully grown. They prefer one another's company, since they are too old to ride on their mothers' backs and too young to move to a new troop. When larger, these males may leave the troop and join another one where they may find mates. The females always stay with their own troop.

Have you seen monkeys combing through each other's fur with their fingers? This is called "grooming." Lemurs

A male ringtailed lemur marking a tree

groom each other. But they use their teeth instead of their fingers. Their lower front teeth have grown together and flattened out into what is called a "toothcomb." Lemurs use these toothcombs to keep their coats and skins clean.

Ringtailed lemurs of all ages like to play. Their favorite game seems to be a quiet rough-and-tumble wrestling match. One animal may sneak up on another and leap on its back. If on the ground, the pair may roll and fight for several minutes. If the lemur that is attacked is in a tree, the battle will not be so even. The victim has to use both hands and feet to hang onto the tree limb. The attacker can use one or more hands to pull the fur and tail of the animal being attacked.

Most kinds of lemurs seem to love the sun. But the ringtail is known in Madagascar as a "sun worshipper." These animals will find a sunny spot where they can sit. They lean back, sometimes against a tree trunk, hold their arms out to the side, and let the full warmth of the sun fall on their bellies. Their eyes close. Their heads sag. Only their ears are up and moving, listening.

Ringtailed lemurs sunning themselves

Chapter 4
Other Kinds of Lemurs

There are about twenty or so different kinds of lemurs still alive in the world. Some of these have been studied carefully. But much remains to be learned by the scientists who are trying to save them.

Ruffed Lemurs

The ruffed lemurs are probably the most beautiful of all. There are two kinds of ruffed lemurs.

The red ruffed lemur has a two-foot-long body that is covered with thick fur that is a deep, rusty red color. Its tail is a little longer than its body, and is covered with thick, black fur. All four feet are also black. The faces of

A red ruffed lemur in typical lounging position

these animals are black with a white nose and a white patch of fur on top of the head. Because of the long, red ruff around the black face, their golden eyes appear larger than they are.

Black-and-white ruffed lemurs are close relatives of the red ruffed lemurs. They are both about the same size, weighing about six to seven pounds when full grown. The body of the black-and-white ruffed lemur is mostly white. It has black patches on the arms and back, and a black tail. A large white ruff frames the black face.

Both kinds of ruffed lemurs in the wild are believed to live in very small family groups. It is rare to see more than three of these animals at the same time. Unlike most other baby lemurs that ride on their mothers, ruffed lemur babies are tucked away in a nest high in the trees.

Most lemurs have calls that sound like grunts, squeaks, or mews. Not so with the ruffed lemurs. They have a loud, angry-sounding call that they make at the least disturbance. This call is used to mark the animal's territory and to sound an alarm.

Both kinds of ruffed lemurs live in the forests along the

A black-and-white ruffed lemur

eastern coast of Madagascar. However, they do not live together, since both kinds eat the same food. If they lived together, there would not be enough food. They seem to prefer fruit, which they often pick and eat while holding it in their hands.

Indris Lemurs

The largest lemur found on the earth today is the indris. Only a few of these animals still live in the eastern rain forests of Madagascar. A full-grown male indris may be nearly three feet long and weigh more than fifteen pounds. Their size, and the howling choruses they make, have caused the indris lemurs to be called "dogs of the forest."

Like the ruffed lemurs, the indrises live in family groups rather than in large troops. A family usually is made up of a female and a male, and several offspring of different ages. Indris babies take several years before they are old enough to leave and start their own families.

The youngsters like to jump on each other and wrestle, but the adults never do. About the only touching

Madascar has issued lemur postage stamps as one means of saving these animals. This one shows indris lemurs. At one time Madagascar was called Malagasy.

adult indris lemurs do is during grooming each other with their toothcombs.

As is true of most other lemurs, the female indris is head of the family. The males, being larger and stronger, will do the fighting when it is necessary. But the mother and older female children always get the first choice of food and branches on which to sit.

These lemurs are active only during the day. They are almost always searching for food. This may be because they are so large and require a lot to eat. They spend very little time resting.

The indrises are rarely seen on the ground. Most of their time is spent very high in tall trees. They seem to

like to be about forty feet above the ground. There they eat several kinds of fruit and young leaves. Once in a while, they eat flowers.

The few indris lemurs that still live in Madagascar may not be able to survive much longer. The forest in which they live is being cleared for lumber and farmland. Unlike most other lemurs, however, the indris is not in much danger from human beings. Many of the people in Madagascar are hesitant to kill the indris because of two superstitions about the animals.

One of these stories says that many years ago, a man and a woman lived in the forests. They had many children. Some of these children began to clear the forest and raise rice. These became human beings. But the other children stayed in the forest where they gathered fruits, nuts, and leaves. These became indris lemurs. Many natives of Madagascar still will not kill indris lemurs because they believe they are "brothers."

The other superstition also protects the indris. Many natives believe that a spear thrown at an indris will be caught and thrown back.

An infant male black lemur on top of his mother

BLACK LEMURS

The black lemur is unusual because the males and females are different colors. Adult males are black and have lots of fur around their heads. The females don't look much like the males, except for their size. Both the males and females are more than two feet long and weigh

about five pounds. But the female black lemur is mostly reddish-tan. Her arms are lighter in color than her body. Her head is dark from the neck up. The hair around her face is white and looks like sideburns.

All baby black lemurs are born with dark-colored fur. As they grow older, the females slowly change color.

Black lemurs live only in the forests near the northeastern corner of the island of Madagascar. Here the forests are still thick and the animals spend very little time on the ground.

They live in small groups of nine or ten animals each. There are usually a few more adult males than females in the group. Groups seem to feed separately during the day, but will often spend the night together with several other groups.

Red-fronted Lemurs

Red-fronted lemurs are about the same size as black lemurs. Females have a tan-colored fur. Males have a slate-gray body, but have reddish eyebrows. As in the case of other lemurs, the tail is used for balance as they

A group of red-fronted lemurs

walk along the branches of the trees in which they live.

Their yellowish eyes seem larger than they really are because of the white patches above them and a very dark stripe between the eyes. Their ears are very short and rounded, and seem to always be moving.

Red-fronted lemurs in the wild usually live in groups of five to ten adult-sized animals, plus a few young. There are almost always a few more adult females than

males in each group. Young red-fronted lemurs may stay with their group for several years.

Unlike most other lemurs, the red-fronted lemurs do not seem to mind when other groups of their own kind try to feed with them. There are very few fights. Once in a while, one adult will lunge at another or cuff the visitor with one paw. But damage is rarely done.

A group of red-fronted lemurs will move around only during the daytime. They will search for food all morning, and then usually rest in the afternoon. They eat mostly leaves of various plants. They seem to like to spend their time about thrity feet high in the trees and almost never come down to the forest floor.

Sifakas

Another kind of lemur is the sifaka, which is named for its "shi-FAK" call. Sifakas are mostly white, with brown patches on their arms and legs. Tiny black ears stick up through a thick, white crown of hair. Their faces seem small because they are black and nearly hairless.

These lemurs have very long hind legs and can make

A sifaka poses for the photographer

huge leaps from tree to tree. Unlike some other primates, they do not use their arms to swing through the trees. Instead, they land on branches with their feet and use their arms to steady themselves only after they have landed. Some of their leaps have been measured at nearly thirty feet!

Sifaka lemurs live in small groups of four to nine and mostly stay in the trees of the Madagascar forest. They

usually eat leaves and fruit, although some of these animals have been seen eating bark and dead wood during very dry periods.

Sifaka groups stay in home areas of the forest. When a strange group wanders into their feeding ground, a noisy fight may start. The fight is carried on mainly by loud sounds and by one lemur trying to get to a favorite tree before a stranger does.

During the breeding season in early fall, serious fights may occur among the males of a group. During these fights, the sifakas use their teeth and hands against each other. The loser of these battles usually leaves the group and joins another one.

Mongoose Lemurs

The mongoose lemur is unusual for two reasons. It is one of several kinds of lemurs that are active at night as well as during the day. And mongoose lemurs are very particular about what they eat. In the wild, they have been observed to eat only from about five different plants. They prefer to eat only the nectar of the flowers

A sifaka

of these plants. They either lick the nectar from the flower or carefully tear the flower apart and eat only the nectar-filled base. Once in a while, they will eat fruit and leaves, but they do this only when they cannot get flowers for nectar.

BROWN LEMURS

Brown lemurs are very gentle toward each other. They live in groups of about eight to ten. There are usually more adult females than males in each group.

A brown lemur in a Madagascar forest

While the young brown lemurs love to play rough-and-tumble games, the adults rarely fight. Once in a while they will cuff each other, or one will lunge at another.

CROWNED LEMURS

The crowned lemurs live only in the dry forests at the northern tip of Madagascar. Like the ringtails, they travel mostly on the ground, but they do eat fruit and leaves in the trees.

The size of a small cat, the crowned lemur weighs

A female crowned lemur with a female infant

about four pounds. The body is about a foot long and the tail is about eighteen inches long.

Female crowned lemurs are gray with a white belly. They have a reddish V-shaped crown of fur on their heads. Males are reddish-brown with lighter bellies. They have a black fur patch on their heads that forms part of the reddish-brown crown.

Like almost all lemurs, the crowned lemur has a good sense of smell. It also is very resourceful. Most lemurs drink from pools on the ground, but crowned lemurs also get the water they need during the dry season by licking dew from leaves in the trees.

A male crowned lemur

Chapter 5
Studying the Lemur

There are two ways scientists can study animals. One way is to go where the animals live and observe them in the wild. The other way is to study animals that are kept in cages or pens. Scientists are using both of these methods to learn more about lemurs.

Going to Madagascar to study wild lemurs is a difficult job. The American scientists must travel halfway around the world to get to the island. And finding the wild lemurs is also difficult. The scientists must follow the groups of animals as they move from place to place looking for food. It is hard to learn to identify individual lemurs unless the scientists can spend a great deal of time with the group.

Scientists know that animals in captivity may not behave the same way as they would in the wild. However, there are advantages in observing an animal in captivity. Here it can be watched all the time. This has been the way scientists have learned much of what they know about lemurs. Their trips to Madagascar are used to study any differences there might be between wild lemurs and those in captivity.

The best place in the world to study captive lemurs is at the Duke University Primate Center where Chiclette was born. It is here that the largest number of lemurs outside Madagascar can be found. Let's take a trip there.

Duke University is located in the rolling hills of central North Carolina. The University owns more than 8,000 acres of woods which are used by the students and teachers for different kinds of study. On ten acres of the Duke forest stands the Primate Center.

We drive down a narrow, gravel road that is shaded by tall pine and oak trees. As we arrive at the Center, we see thick stands of a plant that may seem out of place. It is bamboo, which is one of the favorite foods of several kinds of lemurs.

As we park our car, we are greeted by a startling noise. Some of the lemurs in a wire cage that is shielded by the bamboo have seen us. They greet us with a loud, deep, barking call. Soon the warning spreads. Other animals take up the cry. Some scream with a high-pitched voice. Others cough or grunt loudly. Some make clicking sounds. Others simply squeak. Within seconds, nearly 300 voices are telling each other that a stranger is nearby.

After a brief stop at the reception desk, a guide shows

The Duke University Primate Center

us around the Center. This is not a zoo where visitors can come and visit whenever they want. Too many visitors might change the way the lemurs behave.

We walk down narrow, rough paths overgrown with bamboo. On all sides are wire cages, each with a few animals inside. Each cage has one or two large milk bottles attached upside down to the wire. Metal tubes run from the bottle to the inside of the cage. These are like the water bottles used to water hamsters or mice.

Many of the cages also contain wooden boxes. These are places where the animals can get out of the weather. This is needed because North Carolina in the winter is much colder than Madagascar. Each box is heated with a red heat lamp like those used in fast food restaurants to keep French fries and other foods warm.

As we stop and look at a family of black-and-white ruffed lemurs, a huge one jumps to the edge of the cage. She looks at us and we look at her. She sniffs with her black nose and opens her foxlike mouth. From it comes a deep bark like the one we first heard when we arrived. A brown lemur in the next cage begins to squeal shrilly.

Next pages: (Left) A mouse lemur, one of the smallest primates in the world. (Right) A dwarf lemur, one of the animals bred at the Primate Center.

Soon the Center is again alive with the warning grunts, clicks, mews, and screams.

These animals are fed Monkey Chow, which is made especially for zoos by the same company that makes Puppy Chow. Most of the lemurs at the Primate Center also get a banana bread called "lemur cake." It is sugarless and contains needed oil and vitamins. All of the lemurs here are also fed fresh fruit and vegetables. Peaches and nectarines are the favorites.

Some of the lemurs at the Center are fed leaves. The sifaka lemurs eat several different kinds of leaves. But they must have mango leaves—about 1,000 each week! These leaves are gathered in Florida and shipped to the Center every week. Of course, all leaves and fruits and vegetables are washed carefully before they are fed to the animals.

Around the bend in the path we find a very large area that is surrounded by a high wire fence. This enclosure is different from the others we have seen. It has no top, is one and a half acres in size, and a small building with many windows stands in its center. On the building, in the nearby trees, and on the ground are dozens of attractive ringtailed lemurs.

A young woman is about to enter the enclosure. Her name is Linda Taylor. She is one of the scientists studying the way the ringtail behaves. She invites us into the cage and tells us about her work.

Each day, she goes into the cage with the lemurs and

A ringtailed lemur inside the enclosure at the Primate Center leaps from one tree to another.

watches what they do. She is watching to see which animals play with each other, which animals are allowed to eat first, and how strange animals are treated by the rest of the troop.

As we talk, several of the lemurs come over to Ms. Taylor. It is almost as if they are saying "Hello" to her. When this is done, the ringtails go back to sunning themselves or nibbling on the leaves of the plants in the enclosure.

All of the lemurs in this cage and in the smaller ones are very healthy and happy in their new home in North Carolina. However, the snow that falls here once in a while still bothers them. They tiptoe carefully through it and can't quite figure out how to climb an ice-covered tree.

Another problem that the scientists at the Primate Center have had to solve was caused by the fact that Madagascar is south of the equator. In the lemurs' natural home, January, February, and March are summer months. Lemurs breed at the end of the summer. In North Carolina, summer ends in October. In order to get

A caretaker feeds a pair of ruffed lemurs on a cold, winter day at the Center.

the lemurs to breed in early November, the animals have to be changed over slowly to the new season.

To do this, animals that are brought from Madagascar are kept inside one of the buildings for a year and a half. The rooms of this building do not have windows. All of the lights are on timers, so that the number of hours of light each day can be controlled. Slowly and gradually the length of the lemurs' days are changed. After about eighteen months, the lemurs are used to having longer days in June and shorter days in December. They are then put into cages out of doors, where they breed when the shorter days of fall come. Their babies are born about three and a half months later.

Few lemurs are brought into North Carolina from Madagascar anymore. It is only when one of the kinds of lemurs is in danger of dying out that the government of Madagascar will allow wild lemurs to be captured and taken out of the country.

Chapter 6
Lemurs of the Past

More than half of all the different kinds of lemurs have already disappeared from the earth. Scientists know a little about these lemurs of the past from the bones they find in North America, Europe, Africa, and other parts of the world.

Most of the kinds of lemurs that have died out were very different from the lemurs that have managed to live to modern times. Many of them were much larger than the lemurs we know today. Some may have been as big as a calf or a large dog. Some of them probably lived in trees, but others may have spent most of their time on the ground.

From a study of the teeth of these lemurs of the past, scientists also believe that their diets were different from modern lemurs. Some of the ground-living lemurs may have climbed trees to eat leaves and fruit. But some of them probably lived on grass, roots, bulbs, and even insects.

Humans are no doubt responsible for the disappearance of many of the larger lemurs in Madagascar. The

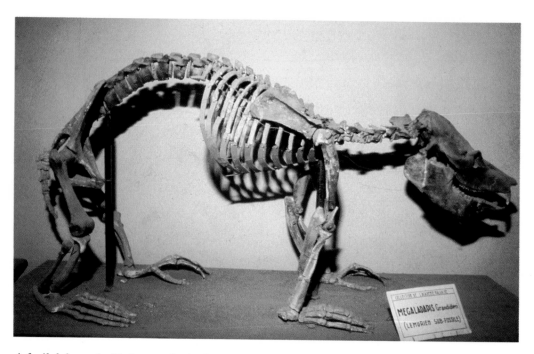

A fossil skeleton of a Madagascar lemur that was as big as a large dog. Scientists learn about lemurs of the past by studying the bones of fossils.

big animals would have been easy to kill with snares, traps, or by throwing rocks or spears. They were probably killed for food.

The human beings that came to Madagascar about 2,000 years ago also needed land for farming and for grazing their cattle. They probably slashed through the bark of the trees and then, after the trees died, cut them down or set fire to them. The lemurs that lived in these

Dr. Elwyn L. Simons, Director of the Primate Center, and fossils found in Egypt of animals believed to be ancestors of lemurs and other primates.

forests are believed to have slowly disappeared as their homes were destroyed.

In 1983, an almost-complete skeleton of an unusual lemur was discovered in a Madagascar cave. This animal was nearly as large as a Boxer dog. It was almost three feet long. It had no tail. And its arms were much longer than its hind legs.

But the strangest thing about this lemur of the past was its hands and feet. Instead of the humanlike fingers of most modern lemurs, it had large, curved fingers. Scientists think these claws show that this animal probably hung upside down from tree limbs, much like modern-day tree sloths. The animal probably was helpless on the ground, but would have gotten along very well in the trees.

The skeleton was found in a narrow cave partly filled with rocks and mud. It was lying under an opening in the roof of the cave. Several of its bones were broken, so scientists think that it probably fell into the cave from a tree limb.

Chapter 7
Lemurs in the Future

What does the future hold for the interesting and beautiful lemur?

At least twenty different kinds of lemurs have died out completely. Will the lemurs still alive today also disappear from the earth?

The government of Madagascar does not want this to happen. Several parks have been set up on the island to protect the homes of the lemurs. Within these game preserves, it is illegal to cut down trees or to kill lemurs.

But many of the people of the island still do not realize how important it is to protect the lemurs. Many think of these animals much in the same way as many of us think of squirrels. They are pests that raid the farmers' grain fields. They are food that can be easily hunted with guns and rocks. The forests that give the lemurs food and shelter are more valuable as farmland than are the animals.

Madagascar is a poor country. Its population is growing rapidly. Within twenty-five years there will be twice as many people on the island than there are today. And in forty years, there may be four times as many.

To feed its people, Madagascar must have more and more food, and this means more farmland will be needed. Also, timber is sold to get money needed to buy things from other countries. With heavy machinery, the forests can be cut down even more quickly than before. The size of the forests is getting smaller and smaller.

The black-and-white ruffed lemur is becoming more and more rare. Close relatives of the sifakas and the gray gentle lemurs are dying faster than babies are being born.

Many scientists are afraid that it is already too late to save the wild lemurs in Madagascar. They believe that

A male gray gentle lemur

within the next hundred years, all of the wild lemurs will have disappeared from the island. If this happens, the only chance the lemur has lies in the work at the Duke University Primate Center and at other places where lemurs are being bred in captivity. There, perhaps, a few of each kind of lemur will be kept alive and healthy, and encouraged to give birth to more of their kind.

Perhaps someday the forests of Madagascar can be regrown. If so, the lemurs raised in captivity can be sent back home to live in the wild forests from which they were taken. If not, perhaps these beautiful little animals will be found only in captivity, like those we visited in the North Carolina forest.

Index

NORMAN D. ANDERSON is Professor of Science Education at North Carolina State University in Raleigh. WALTER R. BROWN lives in Virginia Beach, Virginia, where he taught junior high school science for several years.

In doing research for this book about lemurs, they made several visits to Duke University's Primate Center in Durham, North Carolina. There they were able to observe one of the largest colonies of lemurs found outside of Madagascar, and to talk with the scientists who are studying this interesting group of primates.

Both Dr. Anderson and Dr. Brown received their Ph.D.'s in science education at Ohio State University and they have been writing books together since their graduate student days. They are coauthors of a science textbook series that is used in middle and junior high schools throughout the country. They have also collaborated on *Halley's Comet*, *Fireworks: Pyrotechnics on Display*, and other titles for young readers.